Ipswich
in old picture postcards

by Paul Fincham

European Library   ZALTBOMMEL/THE NETHERLANDS

GB ISBN 90 288 3406 0

© 1986 European Library – Zaltbommel/The Netherlands

Third edition, 1999: reprint of the original edition of 1986.

INTRODUCTION

The Victorians and Edwardians were enthusiastic collectors. James Pope-Hennessy's biography of Queen Mary, George V's consort, recounts how the younger members of the royal family *...loved to accumulate small objects – bronze, stone or china animals, shells, minute vases, little watercolours of gardens, or of Windsor Castle in the mist, a myriad velvet-covered photograph frames containing tiny pictures of each other, their horses and their dogs.* For their less well-endowed contemporaries, picture postcards provided an acceptable substitute. With postage costing ½d (doubled after 1916, but still only 1d), and the cards themselves not very much more, even the modest wages earned by shop assistants, or by girls living away from home 'in service', allowed them to keep in touch with friends, or to let the family back home know how they were liking their new places.

Perhaps because of the nature of the correspondents, and the standards of education at the time, messages written on a collection of cards like this are often disappointingly meagre, or even facetious. One imagines a good deal of head-scratching and pencil-licking, to produce even sentiments of the 'I-hope-this-finds-you-in-the-pink-as-it-leaves-me-at-present' kind. Some of the cards propose or confirm arrangements to meet. Others give travel details. A few are tantalising: No. 129, for example, is one of several written, in a good hand, using a highly elaborate code, obviously carefully worked out and agreed upon by the correspondents, a man and a girl.

For us, a century later, the principal excitements are the pictures themselves, conjuring up as they usually do memories of vanished, or radically changed streets and buildings. Memory, on the whole, is short, and when something disappears, it is very quickly forgotten. Ipswich has seen much change since the end of the Second World War. Clearance of the congested Rope Walk district, which had been a prosperous suburb but became a slum, produced an empty space in the 1930's. Since the War, the whole area has been filled by the Suffolk College and various local-government buildings. More recently, 'rationalising' the traffic-flow around the Dock area has meant large-scale replanning of whole streets, so that the lower parts of Fore Street and Quay Street have lost much of their residential and pedestrian character and convenience. When it was agreed to expand Ipswich in the late 1950's, more wholesale demolition and reconstruction was carried out at the other end of the town: Princes Street, and St. Nicholas and St. Matthew's Streets. That expansion never took place, and the areas which had prepared for it carried for years an unhappy and unfinished look. In the 1970's, the coming of the exciting Willis Faber office-building, and others nearby, corrected the town's balance and redressed some of the mistakes made through anticipation.

In the town centre, the line of Carr Street, Tavern Street and Westgate Street, the town's most ancient thoroughfare, has had its pedestrian functions strengthened and enhanced: after a century, it remains little changed except in the appearance of individual buildings. Some of the old-established shops, like Footmans and Corders, have either changed their shape totally, or have given way to smaller, more ephemeral, boutiques, which seem to change hands (and looks) with an unfortunate frequency. It is reassuring to find some changes for the better. Ipswich learnt the worth of its solid Victorian buildings just in time, and kept its Town Hall and Corn Exchange. The Ipswich Society works tirelessly to encourage the preservation of what is valuable, and to save what is threatened. In the 1980's, paving over part of the Cornhill and partially excluding traffic from the town centre and – most important – from Lloyds Avenue and its arch on to the Cornhill has given the town a more human and more agreeable atmosphere, and one can look at these old pictures with nostalgia, but without too much regret for past times. Interpreting the street scenes, and the civic occasions, has been made easier by reference to the local newspapers. Both the *Ipswich Journal* and the *East Anglian Daily Times* are stored on microfilm among the splendid and readily accessible resources of the Suffolk Record Office, in County Hall at Ipswich.

I have to acknowledge, as on other occasions, the great help and kindness of the Wilton family. The late Mr. Harry Wilton was a knowledgeable collector of Ipswich material. Others besides me must miss being able to talk with him, checking the conclusions they have arrived at, and having their mistakes gently corrected. His widow, Mrs. Gladys Wilton, and his nephew, John Wilton, reacted with characteristic generosity when I tentatively suggested that they might allow me to use his postcard collection. The greater part of the pictures used here come from his albums, where many of the cards have Harry's invaluable notes pencilled in their margins.

Hugh Moffat has been equally kind in letting me use material collected by his father, who succeeded William Bantoft as Town Clerk of Ipswich. His reminiscences, passed on to his son, and now retailed to me, feature in the captions to some of these pictures.

Geoff Cordy, of Felixstowe, has once again, and with unfeigned pleasure, taken on the task of copying, and indeed improving, the original postcards, to ensure the best possible reproduction in the finished book.

Norman Scarfe, as always, has given constant advice and help, demonstrating the most profitable lines of enquiry to pursue, and tempering my over-enthusiasm!

1. The present Town Hall (1868) and on the left the Post Office (1881), with Grimwade's new premises of 1904, dominate the Cornhill in this Edwardian photograph. The electric trams, recently introduced in 1903, have not yet totally replaced the old horse-drawn cabs. These new buildings replaced a group which had proved quite inadequate for the prosperous and expanding town of Ipswich.

2. The earlier Town Hall, an ancient building, had been re-fronted and extended in 1818 to look like this, but it was still unsatisfactory for the administration of the busy town. Together with the adjoining premises of the Corn Exchange Tavern, and R.S. Cole's jeweller's shop, it was demolished in 1865 and the new one built on the larger site.

3. This old Corn Exchange, much rebuilt, was replaced in 1881 by the Post Office. It was often used for concerts and public meetings, in spite of its poor acoustic. When the present Corn Exchange was built behind the Town Hall, this prominent site became available for the Post Office. The figure of Ceres from the pediment is still in the museum's collection.

4. The flamboyant red-brick and stone Lloyds Bank was built, facing the Town Hall, in 1890, four years before this photograph was taken. To the left, the National Provincial Bank building is now part of Debenham's store. The spire of the town's 'civic' church is screened by Tavern Street shops. In 1895, the cabmen's shelter was removed, although it had only been put there two years before. The men lurked inside in bad weather, ignoring customers. It is now in Christchurch Park.

5. The Cornhill about 1910. Electric trams had been running since 1903, but traffic was still largely horse-drawn, and the drinking-trough at the street-lamp's base was much in demand: it was only removed in 1928. Palmer's premises, just left of centre, are still there. Most other Tavern Street façades have changed or disappeared, including the distinctive Picture House cinema, opened that year, 1910.

6. Two public houses – The Sickle and The King's Head – and several small shops and offices were sold (in Lots) and demolished in 1879 to make room for the new Corn Exchange. Building operations were difficult: the site had many old wells which needed filling with concrete. When the building was finished, the old name of King Street became Princes Street.

7. The handsome new Corn Exchange (now a civic Entertainments Centre) was opened on 26th July 1882, when the Mayor, Frederick Fish, gave a dinner for 600 people. This lasted five hours and was followed by a firework display. The Corn Exchange and Town Hall now made an impressive entrance to the heart of the town for people arriving from the railway station, along Princes Street.

8. This 1888 view of the north side of the Cornhill shows the two shops which made way for the big new Lloyds Bank building in 1890. On the right, Bales, the gunsmith (with a target on its roof) is still there, but no longer a shop. At the extreme left, where figures stand round a street-lamp, is the entrance to Mumford's Passage, from the Cornhill up to Tower Ramparts.

Westgate Street, Ipswich.

9. Westgate Street in the 1920's. This was always one of the principal shopping areas. At the left is the entrance to the Public Hall (see No 133), its site now occupied by shops. Just beyond, J.W. Howard was the town's leading photographic studio. Marks and Spencer's store has replaced the row of shops on the right of this picture.

10. Tavern Street was always the main shopping street in Ipswich. The White Horse Hotel (right) and the buildings beyond it were pushed back for road-widening in the early 1800's. The opposite side remained as it looks here until 1929. People still remember how, in the time of the trams, there was not space enough for a carriage or motor car to squeeze between the tramcar and the kerb.

11. The distinctive shape of Frederick Fish and Son's large drapery store is retained, modified, in the present Boots' shop on the corner of St. Lawrence Street. The roller-shutter on the left conceals the International Tea Company's grocery shop, next door to one of the two Ipswich branches of the rival Maypole Dairy Company.

12. The narrow west end of the Buttermarket, clearly seen here, was opened up by rebuilding almost everything between Dial Lane and Princes Street. The shops on the right of this picture have been given modern windows but their upper storeys are hardly changed. The famous Ancient House, with its seventeenth-century front, was splendidly restored in 1985. It is now a bookshop.

13. Upper Brook Street after widening in 1907. The Fox Inn survived into the 1970's. The narrow shop next door, with projecting oriel window, may have been part of the adjacent Coach and Horses Inn, whose upper parts and dormer windows remain, but whose ground floor, with the fine pedimented doorcase, has gone. The London stage coaches once left from this inn. The stables behind could hold 100 horses.

14. The *Ipswich Journal* newspaper had offices here, at the corner of Princes Street and Museum Street, from 1866 until 1890. The building was then demolished and replaced by Fraser's furniture store. The building on the right, a temperance hotel, has become shops and offices but still has the plaque above its third storey where the word HOTEL appeared.

15. The 'town end' of Princes Street improved greatly at the turn of the century: this photograph of about 1905 shows the imposing building occupied by Grimwade Ridley, wholesale druggists, replaced on this site by the black-glass building of Willis Faber and Dumas. Some of the buildings on the left are not much changed. In the background is Fraser's furniture store. It was burnt down soon after this photograph was taken (see No. 68) but rebuilt on the same spot.

16. Falcon Street in the closing years of the nineteenth century: a view from the Old Cattle Market end. The clothier and jeweller's shop on the corner of Silent Street was also a pawnbroker, whose characteristic sign of three balls can just be seen. The Old Provision Market, right, was demolished in 1897, at about the time when this photograph was taken.

17. At the turn of the century, the date of this photograph, the shops at the corner of Falcon Street and St. Nicholas Street, were about to be demolished. The group beyond remains, dilapidated, in 1986. So does the further group, where Boyce the plumber's advertisement can be seen. The neat railings and lamps, and the Congregational Chapel whose entrance they guarded, have made way for a car-park.

18. The trees and railings in this 1890's view of St. Nicholas Street were replaced shortly afterwards by the villas of Cromwell Street, which in turn came down to create Franciscan Way. William Brown, timber merchants, had their premises behind the gates on the left. The dignified house on the extreme left belonged to a solicitor, Mr. Robert Hill. The buildings on the right, and in the background, have not altered their appearance much.

19. A late-nineteenth century view of a group of medieval houses in Silent Street, showing the massive carved corner-post which still stands, at the junction with St. Nicholas Street. The premises continued as a chemist's shop, later known as the Wolsey Pharmacy from its nearness to Cardinal Wolsey's reputed birthplace, across the street. The plaster coat has been removed, and the timber-framing exposed, but this whole group is still easily recognisable.

20. St. Peter's Street, the principal route to the dock and riverside, photographed before 1903 when the introduction of electric tramways made road-widening necessary. All the buildings on the right were rebuilt and set further back. Those on the left, of the sixteenth, seventeenth and eighteenth centuries, are little changed. The Rose, no longer an inn, still has its prominent lamp. Warehouses fill the skyline behind St. Peter's Church.

Bridge St. & St. Peter's St., Ipswich.

21. The Crown Inn and Beckett's confectionery shop dominated the other end of St. Peter's Street, here widened and with tram-rails laid. Gertrude, who sent this card to her friend May, in service at Shrubbery Farm, Otley, on 12th July 1906, wrote: 'Your mother told us that you are collecting postcards. I will send you some views of Ipswich.'

22. A 1908 postcard shows Wolsey's Gate much overgrown with greenery. The gateway, with Henry VIII's royal arms above, is all that remains of the college Cardinal Wolsey was founding in his home town when he fell from power. The building materials were sent back to London for the king's use. As usual, the photographer attracted a small audience of children, who were useful in giving a scale to his picture.

THE
HALF MOON & STAR
HOTEL.
BBOLD'S FINE ALES & STOUT.
'INES & SPIRITS.

LKINSON. HALF MOON & STAR HOTEL.

BARRACK CORNER   IPSWICH

23. Richard Dykes Alexander, a banker and a leading philanthropist in Victorian Ipswich, lived in this sturdy house at Barrack Corner. So, afterwards, did his nephew William Dillwyn Sims, of the firm of Ransome, Sims and Jeffries; and Sims' widow still lived there in 1912, the approximate date of this picture. The house survives, squeezed against the four-storey telephone exchange of 1955. Burlington Road and other nearby streets were made from the gardens of the Alexander house.

24. St. Matthew's Street, looking from Barrack Corner, soon after the end of the First World War. The Queen's Head public house on the corner of St. Matthew's Church Lane has been rebuilt, and the lane itself replaced by Civic Drive. 'Improvements' of the 1960's have involved much demolition in this district, including the shops on the right here: tea-rooms, fancy repository and hosier. Those on the left still stand, though dilapidated, in 1986.

25. St. Matthew's Street, looking from Hyde Park Corner. The big draper's shop on the left – Smith's, Albion House – and the little ones adjoining it (grocer, bootmaker and tobacconist) have given way to Tesco's large store. Of those further on, some parts of the upper storeys are still just recognisable. To make St. Matthew's Street a dual carriage way in the 1960's, the whole of the right hand side was pulled down and the new shops set much further back.

26. The railings are gone, and cars now park on these neat front gardens, but Berners Street today has the urbane look it had in the 1880's when it was relatively new. It leads up to the former East Suffolk Hospital. Several houses were owned by doctors; others by other professional people. The first on the left, with the columned porch, was for many years the residence of Ipswich's Medical Officer of Health, Stanley Hoyland.

27. Hyde Park Corner. Churchman's tobacconist shop was here from 1790 until the firm moved to larger premises in Portman Road in 1898, leaving only the shop. Ipswich's old West Gate stood here until sold for demolition in 1781, at the approach to Westgate Street (ahead, right). Crown Street (left) is much changed. The Rainbow Tavern, at the left-hand corner, came down in the 1960's road-widening scheme.

28. These ancient cottages, on a raised path in Stoke Street, had seen better days. They disappeared in 1899, when the People's Hall was built on the site. Mid-nineteenth century Ipswich had a high death-rate. There was no drainage or sewerage system, and few houses had water laid on. Many were built in 'courts' or 'rows', where several houses shared such facilities as there were.

29. Museum Street, about 1900. The porch on the right (now removed) and the massive columns, fronted the old Museum, purpose-built in 1847, in this handsome new street designed by the Ipswich architect Christopher Fleury, who lived in it himself. The sign between the two substantial houses says *Ipswich Journal,* and the newspaper offices were here from 1890 until publication ceased in 1902. A modern building occupies that site.

11, St. Margaret's Plain, Ipswich.

30. This postcard was produced as his trade card by Harry Walters, photographer. His red-brick house has hardly changed, though his signboard has gone. Canes Café, until lately the Running Buck Inn, and once very popular with farmers, has lost its dormer windows. The group of Tudor buildings on the right, where Soane Street joins St. Margaret's Plain, was once the Packhorse Inn, housing the servants of guests staying at Christchurch Mansion.

31. The Old Manor House on St. Margaret's Green has lost the railings and romantic creeper-cladding of this late Victorian photograph. In the un-ivied part, Margaret Catchpole, known for her smuggling associations, worked for the Cobbold family in the 1790's. The premises of Long the accountant beyond, retain their shape but have lost their plaster coat. Until the early nineteenth century, a fair was held on this Green each September: from early Anglo-Saxon times this was the Thingstead, where the 'Hundred' met.

32. Norwich Road, where it joins Bramford Road (right) still keeps much of what appears in this 1915 view, including the line of shops built out from a terrace of small houses on the left. The prominent gable and chimney-stack of No. 46, beyond them, is unchanged. Much of the group of shops on the right has been replaced by a large garage and showrooms.

33. These cottages at Whitton have gone, probably to make a turning-circle for buses. The group in the distance, altered and extended, may be the Maypole public house. This road, much straightened and widened, was superseded by a new by-pass in 1985 and is now called the Old Norwich Road.

Ipswich. Chevallier Street. No. 141.

34. As Ipswich spread further west, All Saints parish was created from parts of Sproughton, Bramford and St. Matthew's: the church was finished in 1887. Chevallier Street (after Dr. Barrington Chevallier, twice Mayor and Medical Superintendent of the Borough Asylum) has been widened. No. 130 Bramford Road, on the right-hand corner, has come down. Clover's nursery garden on the left has given way to a bank and its car-park.

FLOODS IN BRAMFORD ROAD
IPSWICH

35. The sign, 'Tomatoes 4d lb.' at Clover's nursery in the right-hand distance suggests midsummer. This is probably 1910, when there were twice great storms in August, causing floods in this low-lying district. Bramford Road Post Office then occupied No. 153, on the left. The name-plaque, Mysore Villas 1895, is still there, but the three houses beyond it came down to improve the Yarmouth Road, in the late 1920's.

36. Until the 1930's, Fore Hamlet and its continuation as Bishops Hill, were narrow and closely lined with shops and small houses, lived in by workers at Ransome's nearby Orwell Works. Orvis the plumber, and George Cox, butcher, whose sign declares 'Shipping supplied', occupy the corners of Myrtle Road. Both have gone. So has the terrace of houses, and the White Elm public house, on the left-hand side.

37. After a prolonged snowstorm on Boxing Day, 1906, bringing the deepest snow for twenty years, the tramway service almost came to a standstill. Ten employees, some with shovels, posed for this picture on Felixstowe Road. Truckloads of snow were collected, taken to Stoke Bridge, and dumped in the river. The house at the Salisbury Road corner is still recognisable. A garage occupies the end of this terrace now, but trees at Holywells still fill the middle distance.

38. Singleton the Undertaker's imposing offices at No. 73 dominated the lower end of Wood-bridge Road, from their establishment in 1840 to their demolition in the 1970's. 'Hearses (open or closed), Mourning Coaches, Shillibeers and Funeral Broughams' proclaims their advertisement. They were also conveniently close to the cemetery. A block of modern flats, Samuel Court, now fills this site. The right-hand group of shops and houses is little changed.

39. The Albion Mills public house at the top of Woodbridge Road hill was demolished, 1995. An 1885 *Directory* names a miller, not a publican, living there. A garage has swallowed part of the terrace of houses beyond. The Case is Altered Inn, 1913 'Tudor Revival' by J.S. Corder, fills the extreme right of the picture.

THURLOW
CHIMNEY
SWEEP.

CAULDWELL HALL ROAD. No.138.

40. The Ipswich and Suffolk Freehold Land Society, formed in 1849 to help working-class people acquire their own houses, bought part of the Cauldwell Hall estate. This block, with the name-plaque Freehold Terrace 1877, was one of its earliest developments. This 1913 photograph may have been another trade card. It was sent by the owner of the little draper's shop at No. 190 Cauldwell Hall Road, now once again a private house.

Kirby Street, Ipswich.

41. The most remarkable thing about this postcard is the date on which it was written: 4th August 1914. That day, Britain declared war on Germany, but the sender was not concerned with European politics. 'I have got that place at last, at Felixstowe,' she wrote. 'Now say I don't want to work!' Kirby Street is little changed, although the trees on the left have given way to modern houses.

42. The tramline track between Major's Corner and St. Helen's Church, on the right of this 1907 postcard, was not made double until after the First World War. If two tramcars had to pass each other, they could only do so on a loop of rail in the road at this point. The projecting signboard just beyond the church railings advertises the wares of Goffin the grocer.

43. Tuddenham Road, with milk being delivered to No. 51 by Horace Lloyd, dairyman, whose cart proclaims proudly: 'Jersey Cows Kept for Infants and Invalids.' His dairy is the house on the right of the road. The open ground there, between the road and the Old Cemetery, is now built over with modern houses.

STOKE BRIDGE & CHURCH, IPSWICH

44. A bridge here, at Stoke, was washed away by floods in 1818. William Cubitt, chief engineer in the firm of Ransomes, designed this graceful replacement. The tramcar seems to have strayed into a scene of 1818. Cubitt's bridge lasted more than a century: supplanted in 1924 by a distinctive white, arched structure. In the 1980's that was in turn rebuilt and enlarged to improve the enormous traffic flow here.

45. Disfigured here by evergreens, Ipswich's finest Victorian building, the Custom House, cost £4,250 in 1845. The opening firework display was remembered for many years, particularly by the workhouse orphans, invited by Mayor Rodwell to watch from the quayside. They carried a banner: 'Though Poor, Happy and Grateful.' Zeppelin bombs blew out the clock face in 1916. The building, lately cleaned, has recovered its earliest distinction.

46. To make the Wet Dock, in 1842, the river was dammed below Stoke Bridge and replaced by this channel, the New Cut. The original lock soon proved too small and another was built, but the bricked-up entrance and wing walls (right) survive. Pleasure steamers like this, the *Orwell,* sailed regularly to Harwich and Felixstowe from the New Cut landing-stage. The distant buildings are Mason's oil mill at St. Peter's Dock.

47. The new lock, a decade after its completion in 1881. The swing bridge is not yet in place but the pit for it (on the left) is ready. The barge, the *Ethel Edith,* may have belonged to Edward Packard, whose fertiliser works, along with Ransome's Orwell Works, were in Duke Street. The Ipswich Gas Light Company built their gasworks here in 1822, convenient for importing coal before the railway age.

48. When the Wet Dock was built in the 1840's, the bank of the New Cut was laid out as a public Promenade. A long avenue of lime and pine trees led to the 'Umbrella', a shelter with seats, at the end, from which there was a fine view of the river. Although it was temporarily restored in 1922, the Promenade's amenity-value has been sacrificed to crude commercial interests.

Ipswich. The Promenade

49. A guidebook to late-nineteenth century Ipswich said of the Promenade: *These lines of trees and gravelled paths are delightfully pleasant on a summer evening, especially when the moon is on the waters, and the foliage adds much to the attractiveness of the river itself. No one should visit Ipswich without taking the walk from Stoke Bridge to the Umbrella.*

50. The river and fore-shore were always used for recreation. Water-sports and regatta days drew great crowds. Hog Highland, the site of factories and the former Cliff Quay Power Station (demolished early 1990s), was popular as a children's paddling place. The trees of the Promenade are in the centre of this picture, and the main river channel to the left.

IPSWICH, OSTRICH AND RIVER ORWELL.

39 P.

SMITHS

51. Wherstead was just far enough from Ipswich to make it an attractive place for an excursion. One guidebook remarked: *The Ostrich is a favourite house of refreshment for people strolling on a country walk as well as for persons enjoying themselves in pleasure-boats on the river. There are what are called Tea Gardens attached to the house, but not much tea is drunk, the usual sources of enjoyment being beer and tobacco.*

52. Until almost 1930, the only alternative public bathing place to the Fore Street baths (1894) was on a part of the river bank at Stoke. This postcard was sent to a girl in July 1903 by her brother, presumably one of the swimmers in the photograph. 'I am sending you this as I know you like something spicy,' he wrote. 'If you look closely you will see someone you know, but don't look too close!'

53. Stoke bathing place, being part of the river, was subject to high tides and flood damage: here, the wooden bathing-huts have been tumbled about and smashed. No date exists for this picture but it could well be 23rd November 1908, when an abnormally high tide coincided with a heavy gale.

54. Ipswich proudly celebrated three major new public works on 27th July 1881. Only a month earlier, and perhaps even more important for the town's well-being, a new sewer was completed. Members of the Corporation and their guests sat down to luncheon in a covered reservoir at the works.

55. The cattle market, established in the town centre in 1810, was moved in 1856 to a large new site on the Portman Marshes, alongside the new road – Princes Street – linking the town with the new railway station. The ground was raised three feet above the marsh level in the hope of avoiding flooding. The firm of Robert Bond & Sons, whose advertisement can be seen, conducted regular livestock auctions on the spot.

56. At Orwell Works, Ransome, Sims and Jeffries had thirty acres of ground, and employed 'some 3,000 men and boys in the manufacture of steam engines of all kinds, both for industrial and agricultural purposes', according to a 1912 *Directory*. Here are some of them, at dinner time, in the first years of this century. Packard's Chemical Manure Works (later Fisons) are on the right.

57. Footman, Pretty and Nicolson's factory at Tower Ramparts, built in 1881 and dilapidated in 1986, was still new when this picture was taken. The ridge where the cottages stand is part of the town's old earthen wall. The whole of the foreground area here is now the Corporation's central bus terminus.

Central Premises Carr St

58. Ipswich Co-operative Society's grand new building in Carr Street, built 1885-86, stands on the site of Betts' stables, starting-point of the old London stage waggons. The Tudor house on the left, on Cox Lane corner, was sold, dismantled and removed in 1908 for additional Co-operative Society premises. It was exhibited in London, rebuilt in Northamptonshire, and then destroyed by fire.

59. The terrace of tall mid-nineteenth century houses is still there, in Fonnereau Road (once called Dairy Lane), but this 1911 photograph shows the baker's shop and tearoom which has quite vanished. The hand-cart, and the trade bicycle with its baskets, were used to deliver bread and cakes throughout the district. A poster to the left of the shop door advertises Poole's cinema in Tower Street, opened in March 1909.

60. The row of neat turn-of-the-century villas making up Cromwell Street, with Leverett's shoe shop on the St. Nicholas Street corner, has been replaced by Franciscan Way, itself now redundant and likely to be paved over as a town square. On the left are the Wolsey Auction Rooms. At the extreme left, just visible, is the Hippodrome Theatre which opened in 1905, a few months before Daisy sent this postcard to her friend, Gertie.

61. An advertisement postcard, sent to a Woodbridge customer in May 1906, announcing the removal of Miss Cullwick's business from the Butter Market to No. 14 Queen Street. Nothing now remains of this row of shops: Queen Street has been much widened. The shop on the left belonged to Samuel Warmisham, who made weighing machines. Beyond it, with the large pendant lamp, is the doorway of Davis' china and glassware shop, which remained there until the 1970's.

Series by the Scottish Photographic Touring and Pictorial Post Card Co., Glasgow.

G. A. HACON

The West End
Fruit,
Vegetable
and
Floral
Mart,

43,
Norwich
Road,
IPSWICH.

62. The big hanging lamps, prominent name-board, painted gable-end and glazed extension at the rear have all gone from this shop on Norwich Road. This 1905 postcard was also produced as an advertisement. The proud owner can just be seen, standing in the doorway on the left. The shop still has its unusually modern curved glass window on the Granville Street corner.

63. Alfred Francis Sawer moved here from his much less ambitious shop on the other side of Norwich Road, seen in picture No. 62. This shop still keeps its easily recognisable shape, although Messrs. Coes, who now own it, have added a tall extension at the back, and plate glass windows replace the ones here. The card was sent to a customer as a receipt, signed with the initials A.F.S.

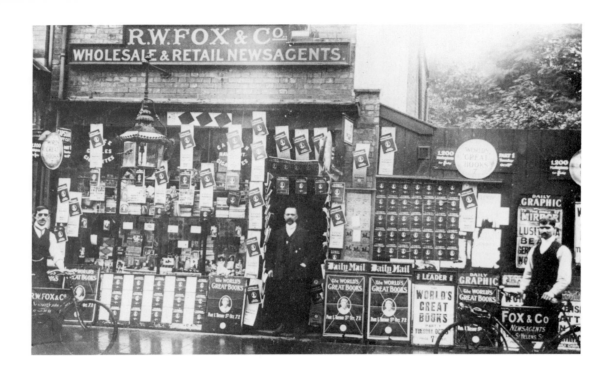

64. 'We thought you would like our other shop', says the message on this 1909 card, sent by the owners to friends at Saxmundham. It was in Fore Street, and the photograph records a special display, advertising a new series, *The World's Great Books*. A fly-sheet behind the man on the right carries news about the *Lusitania*, the ocean liner sunk six years later by the Germans, in the First World War.

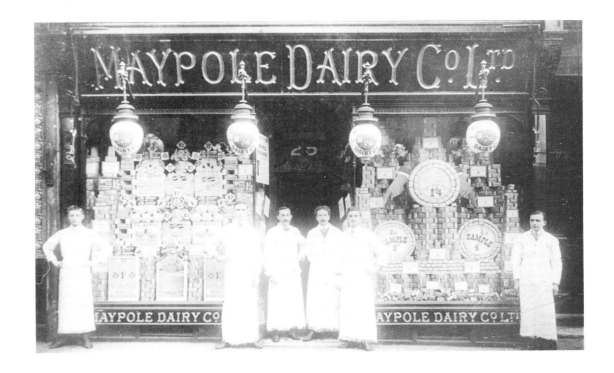

65. The Maypole Dairy Company had a branch in St. Matthew's Street, as well as this one in Tavern Street, photographed in about 1910 by Harry Walters (see No. 30). The boy on the right, Bert, marked himself with a cross before sending the postcard to a young lady. In the right-hand window, tea costs ¼d per pound. The left-hand window-display offers two pounds of margarine for a shilling.

NOTEPAPERS
SMITHS
SUITALL IPSWICH
ACCOUNT BOOKMAKERS
STAMPING
BINDING
MARBLING
NUMBERING
RULING
ACCOUNT BOOKS
STAMPING
SMITHS·SUITALL·IPSWICH.
SHOW ROOMS.
46,48,50, BUTTERMARKET.
SUFFOLK CHRISTMAS SHOW. 1908.

66. An 1885 *Directory* named Mrs. Sarah Smith, stationer, as the owner of a small shop in the Buttermarket. Within a few years it expanded, changing its name to Smiths Suitall. The shop's display at the 1908 trade exhibition suggests a continuing preoccupation with stationery, but contemporary advertisements offer a wide range of goods. The list includes Sheffield cutlery, cutting-out scissors, baskets, grasses, stove ornaments and Gladstone bags.

67. Long after horse-drawn passenger transport had been superseded by motor vehicles, horses were still widely used for delivering goods, especially heavy or bulky items. This is one of the Ipswich Co-operative Society's coal carts, probably in the 1920's. The horse's smart turn-out, including a string of horse-brasses, suggests that the photograph was taken on some kind of festive occasion.

68. When R.D. and J.B. Fraser's furniture emporium, in Princes Street, burned to the ground on 6th April 1912, people questioned whether the town's fire-fighting services, still with horse-drawn engines, were adequate. The fire had seemed to be extinguished, but flared up again later that night. Rolls of linoleum in the furnishing department burned and exploded, spreading the blaze to other shops in that area.

69. Fraser's was one of several disastrous fires in the riverside district of Ipswich at that time. On this postcard, the firemen seem to be standing on the dock embankment, directing their jets at buildings along the quay. Superintendent Wheeler, in command since 1876, retired – perhaps significantly – later in 1912. That year, an appliance with a 50-foot escape ladder was bought. Motor engines were introduced in 1918 and horses eventually abandoned in 1920.

70. The initials on both the mail van and the letter-box in the Post Office portico, E.R., suggest a date of about 1909 for this Edwardian photograph. Motor vans for transporting mail only completely replaced horse or hand-drawn carts in 1926. The figures over the entrance of the 1881 Post Office represent Industry, Electricity, Steam and Commerce.

71. Ipswich Gas Light Company, one of the earliest formed to supply the public with gas, celebrated its centenary in 1921, though this photograph is a decade earlier. The celebrations were at Oak Hill (now part of St. Joseph's College), the Belstead Road home of Sir Daniel Ford Goddard, the company chairman. 'A vast assembly of guests, to the number of over 500,' sat down for tea and speeches in a huge marquee.

72. In the General Strike of May 1926, this group of police officers posed with their emergency vehicle for this picture, in the yard behind the Golden Lion hotel. The postcard identifies them, from left to right, as Jack Fisher, inspector Saunders (on the motor-cycle), Jack Grimwood (driving the tender) and constables Christie, Haylett, Enridge and Pooley. They seem amused rather than perturbed by the occasion.

73. A policeman and a 'Special' constable during the General Strike, seen here returning from the final parade of 'Specials' on 12th May 1926, when the strike had been declared off. The photograph was taken outside Rushbrooke the tailor's shop in Dog's Head Street, looking towards the Old Cattle Market.

74. The East Suffolk and Ipswich Hospital in Anglesea Road opened in 1836, at a cost of £4,148, for fifty patients. It expanded, adding an extra storey and wings and ugly ancillary buildings. Since the Hospital's move to Heath Road, this has been Anglesea Heights nursing-home. Some buildings at the rear, in Ivry Street, were converted, 1996, to the Ipswich School's Pre-Prep Department. John Chevallier Cobbold, who did much for Ipswich, was the Hospital's first Treasurer and Secretary.

75. This photograph of about 1890 shows one of the new wards at the hospital, hygienic but spartan, with iron cots and bed-boxes, plain scrubbed floor and central stove. Pictures on the walls are mostly of an 'improving' kind. Throughout the 1890's, 'Hospital Tuesdays' were held annually each autumn to raise funds. £181 was collected in 1893, but only £86 two years later.

BROADWATER, IPSWICH.

76. Broadwater, on Belstead Road, was used as a military hospital during the First World War. The first wounded arrived on 21st October 1914, the last man left on 6th February 1919. Here a group of soldiers, two with arms in slings, pause for the camera during a game of croquet, while a nurse watches from an upstair window. The house has been demolished, its grounds built over. A lodge may survive as No. 97 Belstead Road.

77. Hope House Orphanage, on the corner of Foxhall Road and Alan Road, opened in 1883 with Miss Hannah Warner as matron. A memorial stone attributes its foundation to Edward Grimwade, Esq., J.P. The rear view of the large brick and terracotta house looks as it does here, except for an extension on the right, and a fire escape. In 1986, it is used as a hostel by the Mental Aftercare Association.

78. The first Ipswich Museum, founded in 1847, soon outgrew its premises in the new street to which it gave its name (see No. 29). 'It is in many respects one of the best provincial museums in the kingdom,' said a local guidebook. This view of the interior, on the eve of its move in 1881, shows display cabinets and showcases which are still being used today in the new, larger building, in High Street.

79. When the collections moved to their new home, the old museum was used by Archer and Turner, a firm of auctioneers and valuers. By 1907 Turner had gone, and H.E. Archer was using the old museum as a ballroom. It was he who sent this postcard to a patron, with the message: 'The Dances for the Season will be resumed on 7th October at the Assembly Rooms, Museum Street.'

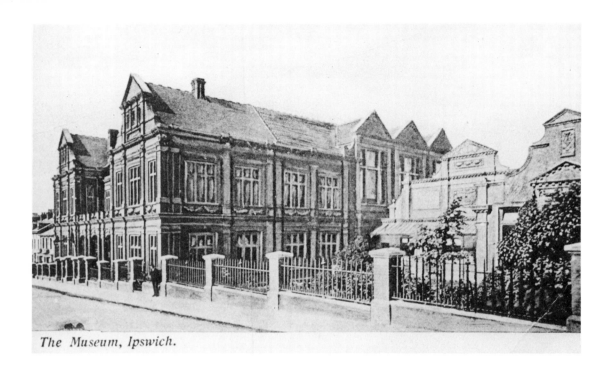

The Museum, Ipswich.

80. The new Museum in High Street, opened in 1881, along with the Post Office and new lock gates (see No. 54), also housed the School of Art and the Free Library. Once again the contents outgrew the premises. The Library was extended in 1887, and a new wing for the Museum was added in 1901. In 1924, the provision of a separate library in Northgate Street released much-needed additional space for the expanding museum collections.

Social Settlement. Ipswich.

81. Ipswich Social Settlement, ten years after its foundation in 1896 by Mr. (later Sir) Daniel Ford Goddard, a good friend to the town, as a non-political and undenominational community centre. Its activities and services were important in the days before the welfare state. It stood, massively, at the lower end of Fore Street, near the most densely-populated part of the town. It was demolished only in the 1950s, as part of a road improvement scheme.

QUEEN ELIZABETH'S GRAMMAR SCHOOL, IPSWICH.

82. Ipswich School, about 1890, before the trees in the Upper Arboretum had grown up to soften the 1850s brickwork. Fonnereau Road and both arboretums were made from the public meadow of Bolton. Some older inhabitants still spoke nostalgically of Bolton, 'without its gravelled paths or shrubs or flowers, without boards up at every turn with cautions to visitors, without lodge keepers closing and opening gates at fixed hours…'

Convent of Jesus & Mary, Ipswich. View from Playground.

83. The Convent of Jesus and Mary, on Woodbridge Road, had one of the town's two Roman Catholic schools. This large building is still there, but seems somehow less impressive, screened by the surrounding buildings, and with modern housing going up on part of its site, fronting Woodbridge Road, opposite the Albion Mills public house (see No. 39).

IPSWICH, MUNICIPAL SECONDARY SCHOOL.

SMITHS

84. The Municipal Secondary School for Boys (by J.S. Corder), on Tower Ramparts, soon after its opening in 1889. Pupils called it the 'Muni'. The large red-brick building, with distinctive curved gables, was demolished in 1979. The site is now filled by the Tower Ramparts Shopping Centre, cutting right through to Tavern Street.

85. The Boys' Middle School, in Bolton Lane, opened in 1885. This photograph was taken by one of the pupils some ten years later. Their motto: 'Well begun is half done,' in Latin, would no longer be understood. The rigid arrangement of desks, the bare walls and high windows, are characteristic of most schools at that period. Flaxman, the school porter, rang a handbell to indicate the time for a change of lessons. This central schoolroom, now much more cheerful, is the concert-room of the County Music School.

86. Great Colman Street, built in the 1820's on the gardens of (Tudor) Harbottle House, was terminated at its Northgate Street end by these Assembly Rooms. They later became a School of Art, Girls' High School, motor works, dry cleaner's, and a stationery shop. The upper part has been extended since this 1890 photograph, and modern shop windows inserted, but the structure is still easily recognisable.

87. This postcard is one of the *Pickwick* Series, recalling Dickens' reference to the Great White Horse Hotel in his book *Pickwick Papers*. The hotel's early nineteenth century façade is deceptive. Its original timbered courtyard, glazed over to make another room, is more easily recognisable for what it is in this photograph of about 1910 than it is today, with more sophisticated fittings and furniture.

The Barracks, Ipswich.

88. 'I need not tell you whose favourite place this is,' wrote Kate to her friend Nell in 1907, on this postcard of the Ipswich Cavalry Barracks. Other contemporary photographs of groups of soldiers explain the establishment's popularity with the Ipswich girls! The Barracks, for 1,500 men, were built in 1796 in St. Matthew's parish. Barrack Corner and Barrack Lane still remind us of them, although the buildings had gone by 1930.

89. The Barracks occupied 9¼ acres, seen in this early aerial photograph, between St. Matthew's Street and Angelsea Road, with Berners Street at the top right. Several inscribed stones, marking the boundary, survive, one built into a garage behind new shops in St. Matthew's Street. The original entrance-gate posts, topped by stone balls, still stand where they always did, in Barrack Lane.

Ipswich. Barracks. Royal Horse Artillery. C. Battery.

SMITHS

90. In 1929 the Council bought the whole site for £8,000 and used it to build Cecil and Geneva Roads. Some of the houses in those roads have, at the bottom of their gardens, those high brick walls which once enclosed the Barracks, with occasional tethering-rings for horses set into them; and here and there the government-property mark of the broad arrow.

91. A new Drill Hall, at the town end of Woodbridge Road, was opened on 13th May 1911.
The first occupants were the men of the 6th (Cyclist) Battalion of the Suffolk Regiment.
Watlings, who supplied the stonework and advertised the fact on this postcard, traded from
Derby Road station. The hall is now the Ipswich Caribbean Association International Community Centre. A garage replaces Garrod Turner & Son's hoarding, on which one poster offers advice about emigration to Canada.

IPSWICH FIELD OF HONOUR.

92. Ipswich Old Cemetery still has the Field of Honour, where a stone records that the first memorials were set up by the Ladies' Guild. They commemorated those killed in the First World War: the first interment was on 3rd August 1915, and there was a special service on the eve of the official Peace Celebrations in July 1919. The obelisk has lost its wirework cross. It is curious that the plot had (and retains) the look of a French, rather than an English, war cemetery.

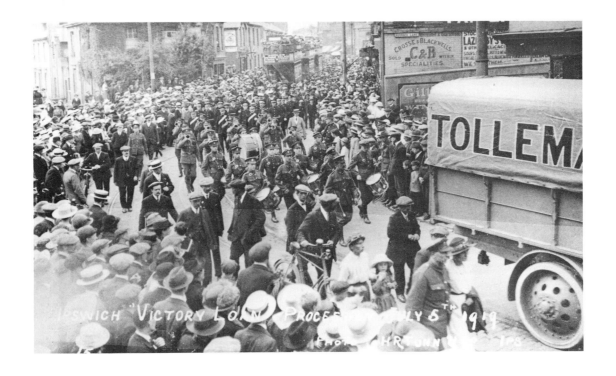

Ipswich "Victory Loan" Proce... July 5 TH 19.. ...R.TUNN... IPS

93. Celebrations in 1919, for the end of the First World War in the previous November, included an attempt to encourage saving through what was called a Victory Loan. On 5th July, 450 schoolchildren took part in an elaborate procession, led by a lorry, decorated by the girls of Clifford Road school to represent Victory. The procession, including five bands, started at Broomhill, a favourite assembly-point. Part of it is seen here at Barrack Corner. Ipswich raised nearly a million pounds in the loan.

LORD KITCHENER ADDRESSING BOY SCOUTS, IPSWICH. 10.

94. Lord Kitchener came to a scout rally on 31st May 1911. 'Portman Road made a splendid rallying-ground,' reported the newspaper, 'and the grandstand was crowded with well-known people.' Kitchener, in blue serge suit and bowler hat, spoke first to the St. John Ambulance nurses (right background). After some swordstick, ju-jitsu and first aid displays, the boys grouped round a flagstaff. 'Photographers were firing at his Lordship without intermission, but he seemed unconcerned.'

Gen. French Unveiling Ipswich B... Memorial. No. 6.

95. The Cornhill, extraordinarily crowded on 29th September 1906, when General Sir John French unveiled the South African War memorial: people even sat among the statues on the Post Office façade. Elaborate traffic regulations were necessary. The sculptor, Albert Toft, 'was conspicuous from his youthful appearance, and from the plainness of his dress' compared with the official party. Traffic over the Cornhill had increased so much by 1931 that the statue was moved to Christchurch Park.

96. The Bantoft family in their garden. William Bantoft was Town Clerk of Ipswich for more than forty years, until he was killed in a motor accident on Bucklesham Road in 1925. This photograph shows the typical well-to-do middle-class Edwardian family, living comfortably in one of the solid new houses in the most salubrious part of the town – Hamilton Tower, on Westerfield Road, facing Christchurch Park. Bantoft himself stands on the left.

97. A calendar on the wall behind him shows that it was 1897 when Mr. Mayes, Town Sergeant, sat still enough in his office in the Town Hall to have his picture taken by a junior. The Council had only a small staff at this period, and the Town Sergeants often took on extra duties, attending evening functions when Mayors held receptions, or when the big rooms in the Town Hall were lent or hired to non-political organisations for meetings.

98. General William Booth of the Salvation Army stopped at Ipswich on 8th September 1905, during a motor tour. At the Workhouse – his first call – the officiating ladies pushed aside the inmates in their excitement. 'Let the workhouse people come forward,' said the General. 'You ladies stand back – you ain't the proper people!' On the Cornhill, Mayor Grimwade greeted his guest at the Town Hall, with the Town Sergeants on either side of the doorway.

99. Mission Sunday, 18th September 1921, resulted from the Church of England clergy's inviting the local Trades Council and Labour Party to an undenominational church service. The newly-appointed bishop, Dr. David, led the procession from Barrack Corner to St. Mary-le-Tower Church, which was packed, mainly with men. Members of the Trade Unions, their banners held high, can just be seen at the end of the procession as it crosses Cornhill.

100. The first Ipswich 'Lifeboat Saturday' was held on 10th July 1897. The procession, 'unsurpassed for variety of detail and the enthusiasm with which it was received', was a mile long. One carriage of eight girls represented the four Seasons. Ipswich Swimming Club contributed 'Father Neptune'. The main attraction, seen here, was the Ilfracombe lifeboat, drawn by eight horses. Its crew wore red caps, blue jerseys and cork lifebelts. It remained on show next day in Christchurch Park.

101. The procession travelled from Broomhill to the dock, through the main streets of Ipswich, marshalled by a large body of police. Along the route, as here at the Cornhill and in Tavern Street, the crowd stood several deep, and every window was occupied. In those days, people regularly 'lived over the shop'. In St. Matthew's Street, one over-excited lady spectator burst the varicose veins in her leg, and was taken to hospital. The organisers hoped for £200, and the event raised £217.

LIFEBOAT SATURDAY

102. In 1907, 'Lifeboat Saturday' was as popular as ever. The Holy Wells Dairy, of 172 Felixstowe Road, entered this milk cart, where a little girl sat with a collecting-box 'for which contributions were invited by a humorous notice on a sheet'. The Ipswich Gas Company's float had a model kitchen, where white-coated chefs were baking. Their placard read: 'If gas ovens don't save lives, they save time and money.'

103. Field-Marshal Viscount Allenby, whose home was at Felixstowe nearby, after he had received the Freedom of the Borough of Ipswich on 6th October 1919. The guard of honour of wolf cubs can be seen on either side: they were afterwards known as Lord Allenby's Own. Mayor Ransome entertained a great many guests to lunch. Local newspapers reported that the crowd on the Cornhill 'cheered again and again when the hero of Palestine arrived in his car'.

104. Bus-shelters and car-parking nowadays make it difficult to see the 1860 railway station as well as we do on this postcard of about 1908. The new electric trams ran between the station and the Cornhill every five minutes, although the principal hotels still sent their cabs to meet travellers. The Station Hotel, right, already advertised that it could provide both 'good stabling' and a 'motor garage and cycle house'.

GREAT EASTERN RAILWAY.

Ipswich G.E.R. Station. 322.

105. The Railway Company ran its own buses between Ipswich and Shotley. Seats on the upper deck had waterproof sheets which passengers pulled over their knees in wet weather. The handsome lamps have gone from the forecourt, but the station building is not much changed since Rifleman Auty sent this postcard to a London girl in 1915, saying: 'I hope you will like this card of the station.'

ELECTRIC TRAMS IN IPSWICH.   A TRIAL TRIP, NOVEMBER, 1903.

106. Electric trams replaced horse trams in 1903. This one, on a trial trip on 10th November, posed for its photograph outside No. 331 Norwich Road (at the corner of Kitchener Road), which was as far as houses then stretched along Norwich Road. Ten days later, the sender of this card wrote, facetiously, of the trams: 'They have only knocked over three milk carts, and killed several men and dogs as yet.'

107. 'Passengers are requested to keep their seats while the car is passing under the bridge,' is the warning painted on Norwich Road railway bridge. The open space beyond is now completely built over: traffic signals, and a right-hand turn into Ashcroft Road, are where the cart stands in the centre of the road. The bridge's two outer arches have been bricked up.

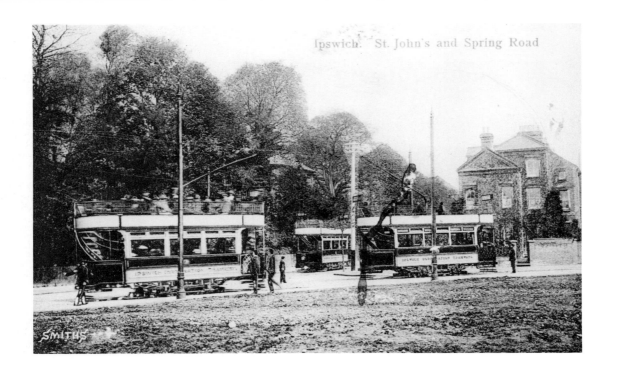

108. The Corporation bought twenty-six tramcars: double-deck, open-top, each seating fifty passengers. Electric current was collected from overhead wires. By December 1903, the service had been extended to Lattice Barn and Derby Road station, forking here at the junction of Spring Road with St. John's Road. The trees on the left now screen blocks of flats. Rutland Terrace, 1894, on the right is unchanged.

The Viaduct, Spring Road, Ipswich.

109. Colonel Tomline of Orwell Park built the railway to Felixstowe. The line, opened in 1877 on May Day, crossed Spring Road on this graceful viaduct, more than sixty feet tall, to reach Derby Road station, which served the town's eastern suburbs. Although the terrace on the left here has not changed, the wall and trees on the right have been replaced by new roads and modern houses.

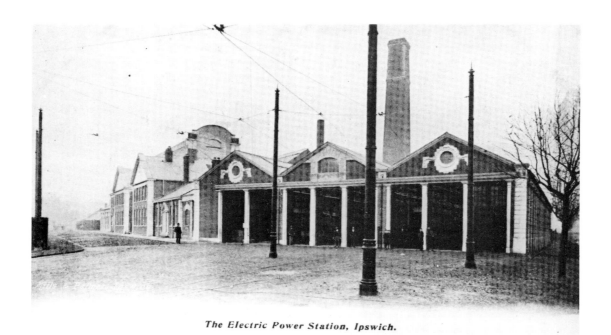

The Electric Power Station, Ipswich.

110. The Electric Supply and Tramway Station was the grand name given to this new building in Constantine Road. The Mayoress opened it on 21st November 1903, entertaining her guests to luncheon and a celebratory tram-ride to the Whitton terminus. The chimney has gone, but the building, although dwarfed by the enormous Ipswich Town Football Club stand, looks much the same.

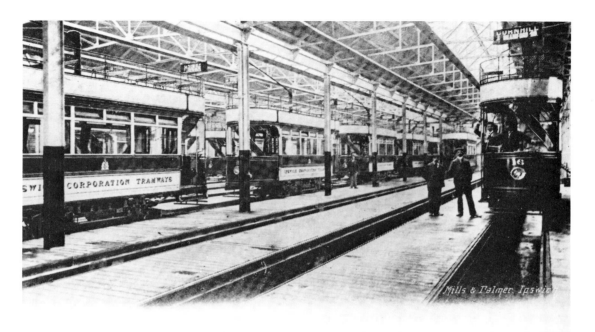

The Electric Car Station, Ipswich.

111. Some of the original fleet of tramcars in their garage which, with the rails removed, Ipswich Corporation buses still use today. The generating station, which was an essential part of the tramway system, also provided electricity for those inhabitants of the town who wanted it. By 1909 there were even a few electric lamps lighting the Ipswich streets.

112. A surgeon and a solicitor occupied these large houses on the left, with gardens running right through to Woodbridge Road, when this postcard of Major's Corner was sent in 1910. Motor-car showrooms, and the Gaumont (originally the Regent) cinema now stand here. The shops on the right (see No. 64) are less changed, though the Mitre Tavern has come down at the far end of the row. The County Hall, of 1837 and 1906, is still in use and looks as good as new with its brickwork cleaned.

113. In 1923, trams were replaced by trackless trolleybuses, made by Ransomes of Ipswich and Garretts of Leiston. Princes Street was one of the first routes used. Here, the old rails are being taken up, while a trolleybus with its open smokers' platform avoids the operations cautiously. The old horse trough and drinking fountain, at the corner of Princes Street and Portman Road, can be seen.

114. Botwood and Egerton's garage in Carr Street (between the Lyceum Theatre and the Gas Showrooms) sent this postcard to an Orford customer in December 1908: 'Dear Sir, we are returning today the tube which you sent us for repairs.' It must have come from a car like the one on show here, with its early registration number of DX 180. The hanging sign advertises Carburine Motor Spirit. Not long after this, Botwood and Egerton moved to Major's Corner.

LONDON — YARMOUTH BYE-PASS ROAD IPSWICH.

115. The council decided in 1923 to by-pass the town from London Road, round its northern edge to Woodbridge Road. The new road was opened on 3rd August 1929. This photograph (by Gillson, of Brooks Hall Road) shows the junction with Graham Avenue, at the foot of Valley Road hill. Westwood Avenue is not yet built. Houses now stand on the slopes where, here, ponies are grazing.

IPSWICH TOWER CHURCH 2702

116. St. Mary-le-Tower, the principal Ipswich church, had looked like this only since 1870, by which date it was almost totally rebuilt, along with its vicarage, on the right. The building on the left, once the lecture-hall of the Ipswich Mechanics Institute, opened March 1909 as Poole's cinema. Three weeks later it was advertising 'The very latest production in Animated Photography, Wilbur Wright's aeroplane flight before the King'. Re-opened, 1947, as the Ipswich Arts Theatre, it was converted most successfully in the 1990s to a pub, The Old Rep.

117. Christchurch Mansion was still overgrown with creeper in May 1904, when Lady Bristol unveiled this memorial to Queen Victoria, on a dismal day. One of every nine Ipswich people had contributed to its cost. The bronze lions were popular with children: the writer remembers being lifted on to the back of one on a very hot day; the metal felt red-hot to bare legs! The statue was melted down, for munitions, in the salvage drive of the Second World War.

118. The Town Council, somewhat reluctantly, bought Christchurch Park in 1894, and Felix Cobbold, M.P., gave Ipswich the Mansion. Next year the park opened to the public, the Mansion in 1896. Christchurch became the favourite setting for most public festivities. In great storms, in July 1902, tons of material were washed down from the top end of the park into the Round and Wilderness ponds, making them overflow. Some of the fish were carried as far as Lower Brook Street.

119. Peace Day was officially on 19th July 1919, ending the First World War. The celebrations in Christchurch Park included aquatic sports, arranged by the Ipswich Swimming Club. Spectators at the Round Pond were packed tightly together, to watch life-saving displays and water polo (notice one of the goals). This picture shows the 'star turn', Harry Calow, who swam round the pond with feet and hands tied together. He also dived into the water with a lighted cigar, and came to the surface smoking it.

120. Christchurch Park's popularity can be judged from the adults and children around the Wilderness Pond in this Edwardian photograph. A man was found drowned in it in 1909. Beyond the pond, the Lower Arboretum at this period was reserved for subscribers, while the Upper, like the park itself, was open free of charge.

Christchurch Park, Ipswich.

Axis Deer, Indian Gazelle, Persian Gazelle.

121. A small collection of animals and birds, including peacocks, was kept in Christchurch Park, to entertain and instruct children. In September 1907, several Fonnereau Road householders (including a Mr. Peecock, from No. 37!) summoned the Mayor and Corporation, saying that the birds had been placed there with the best of motives, 'but their cries constituted a nuisance which had become simply intolerable'. Other residents, however, disputed these allegations, and the case was dismissed.

122. Alexandra Park, named after Edward VII's queen, was opened on 18th June 1904, when Mayor Bennett unlocked its Grove Lane gates with a silver key. The new park was crowded, mainly with children, 'in all the varied hues of their frocks and hats and pinafores', who collected on its slopes to watch a balloon ascent. The ascent was made from fields, lent by the Freehold Land Society, who had not yet built upon them, between the park and St. Helen's Street. The new park was particularly appreciated by people from the nearby Rope Walk district, whose tightly-packed houses allowed no recreation space.

123. St. Helen's Lodge, with the trees of Alexandra Park in the distance, and open ground where the houses of St. Helen's Street have not yet spread as far as Grove Lane. The house was badly damaged by German incendiary bombs in 1942 and was subsequently partly demolished. Only the section nearest to the camera remains today.

GAINSBORO' LANE

124. This 1904 postcard, one of the *Christchurch* series of local views, shows the beauty spot, Gainsborough Lane, which runs down to the River Orwell from Clapgate Lane. The painter Thomas Gainsborough lived in Ipswich (1752-1759). He loved walking, and would have known these banks of the river well. The Council, mindful of its new housing estates on this side of the town, bought the area for recreational purposes in 1926.

Ipswich. Meet of the Hounds in Constable Road, 1902.

125. William Bantoft, Ipswich's first full-time Town Clerk, was Hon. Sec. of the Essex and Suffolk Hunt. His house (see No. 96) was close to Constable Road, largely undeveloped at the beginning of this century. On hunt days he went early to the Town Hall, attended to any important business, then removed his pin-striped trousers to reveal riding-breeches under them. 'If anyone wants me, I'm out with the mayor,' (i.e. the mare!) he explained to his deputy.

126. Holywells, in 60 acres of parkland and lakes, was the home of Felix Cobbold, whose gifts to Ipswich included Christchurch Mansion. In July 1897, seven years before this postcard was printed, a fierce storm damaged the house which was undergoing alterations, with some parts roofed only by tarpaulins. The ground floor rooms were flooded when there was more rain than the drains could carry away. Since 1936, this has been a public park. The house was demolished in 1962, the terrace steps, conservatory and stable block survive.

STOKE PARK.   IPSWICH.

127. An 1885 *Directory* described Stoke Park as a handsome mansion in a well-wooded park of 500 acres, commanding beautiful views of the river. When this card was sent in 1914, probably by one of the housemaids working there, it belonged to Lord Gwydyr, and was a popular place for Sunday School treats and children's outings. The house came down about 1930 but some of these fine trees still stand, among the modern houses of the Stoke Park estate.

128. The River Gipping, as it curves along Ranelagh Road (right). The Station Hotel, and the tall block of Willoughby Terrace, 1888, are seen, just beyond the original wood and iron bridge which linked the town with the railway station. It was replaced by the present stone bridge in 1927. Tall houses were subsequently built on these meadows fronting Ranelagh Road. They have recently been demolished, but the chance of making an attractive riverside here has not been taken.

Ipswich Show. 1907

129. The annual Christmas show for 1907, in an old drill hall near the cattle market, had as its theme 'I dreamt I dwelt in marble halls'. The massive 'marble' columns were made of wood, but the electric lighting was real. All the principal shops had displays at the show, mostly of a seasonal kind, such as 'a tasteful and original table, decorated for a children's Christmas party'. A military band played every day during the show.

130. Barnum and Bailey's circus generated immense excitement when it came to Ipswich in 1898, and again in 1899. 13,000 people packed into the tent, on Bramford Road, for each performance. Half of them were from outside Ipswich, and tales were told of half-empty schools and deserted workshops. The circus arrived from Croydon, its special train using the old railway station 'over Stoke' to cause the least possible disruption to normal services.

131. Ipswich saw Buffalo Bill's Wild West Show in 1903: four special trains, 500 horses, 800 performers, including these 'genuine blanket Red Men'. Bramford Road showground was soft after rain: the waggons sank to their hubs. A cowboy band gave a free concert before each performance. The evening show was brilliantly lighted from the company's own 25 h.p. engines and dynamos. Ipswich talked of little else for the following week.

132. This large gathering in the Public Hall was to celebrate 'Freedom Day', 21st April 1920, when the Freedom of the Borough was conferred on Ipswich men who, in the First World War, had been awarded the D.S.O., the D.C.M. or the Conspicuous Gallantry Medal. On the platform, Mr. F.E. Rands, in his second term as Mayor, addresses the congregation. Those men being honoured are wearing service uniforms. The organist in his gallery is ready to play the national anthem.

IPSWICH. Public Hall, the Organ. 712.

133. The Public Hall, built in 1868, could hold 2,000 people. Electric light was installed there very early, in 1903. The fine organ, from Exeter Hall in London, was rebuilt and installed here in 1907. The hall was used for every kind of entertainment, including moving pictures for a while in the 1920's, but it was a curiously cheerless building, and few were sorry when it burnt down in 1948. The organ was totally destroyed in the blaze.

134. 'The handsomest place of amusement in Suffolk,' was one description of the Hippodrome, opened in St. Nicholas Street on 28th March 1905. This card, posted just a month later, asks the recipient: 'What do you think of this?' and seems to show the opening week, when a team of elephants performed. For fifty years the 'Hipp', which was demolished in 1985, staged pantomimes and regular variety shows before ending its life as a ballroom and bingo hall.

135. The Lyceum Theatre in Carr Street opened in 1891 and closed in 1936. Its life of forty-five years included one decade as a cinema. The turreted building beyond it is the East Anglian Daily Times newspaper offices. The Carr Street shopping precinct, in bleak concrete, now fills that whole site. The substantial house on the left belonged to a leading Ipswich surgeon and physician, F.C. Wetherell, when this card was sent in 1910. Woolworth's store now stands there.

PALACE SKATING RINK
IPSWICH.

SESSIONS:

11 a.m. till 1 p.m.

2.30 p.m. „ 5 „

7 „ „ 10 „

136. The Palace Roller Skating Rink opened, like Poole's cinema (see No. 116) in March 1909, on the site of the Old Provision Market in Falcon Street. It was built, in only nineteen days, of wood and iron, and had a maplewood 'skating' floor, 140 feet by 50 feet. Fourteen large gas lamps provided illumination. 'The attendance, both of skaters and sightseers, was excellent,' said the newspaper, about opening day, but The Palace had a short life. It closed in 1920, and was replaced by the G.P.O. sorting office, opened in 1923.

THE EMPRESS SKATING RINK. IPSWICH.

137. A second roller-skating rink, The Empress, in Portman Road, opened only four months after The Palace. This was a much grander affair, with an orchestra, tea-rooms, gardens, and even a garage among its attractions. Skating races were popular there. On opening night, when 3,000 people were present at one time or another, there was a mile, and also a half-mile, race for gentlemen, and something called a balloon race for ladies. The 'frogged' jackets worn by the men in this group suggest that it may be a staff photograph, perhaps for advertisement.

138. The Ipswich Town football team of 1902: the date is painted on the ball held by the captain. This card was sent to a lady by, presumably, one of the players, who wrote on it the message: 'Do you recognise anyone in this group?' At this time, Ipswich belonged to the Norfolk and Suffolk (amateur) League. Matches were played on a pitch at Broomhill until Portman Road recreation ground opened in 1888.

139. 'This is No. 1 squad of our gym,' wrote George, who sent this card, in the early years of the century. These were members of the St. Matthew's Church Men's Club. The card's message continued: 'The parson in the centre is our fighting parson and a good handful. The one on the right is the Rector of St. Matthew's.' This may therefore be the Reverend William Fletcher, who was certainly rector in 1912, and the photograph was perhaps taken in the rectory garden.

Tobogganing on Constitution Hill.
N°1

140. Like No. 37, this card is one of a series of pictures taken after the great Boxing Day snow-fall of 1906. The big 'family' houses of Constitution Hill, at the top of the town, beyond Christ-church Park, have not changed much, but 1980's traffic would make tobogganing hazardous. The children, who seem to be all boys, are rather formally dressed for the occasion, but collars and caps were more usually worn at that period, even for such an activity as this.